# THE AESTHETIC METHOD
# IN SELF-CONFLICT

# THE
# AESTHETIC METHOD
# IN SELF-CONFLICT

*by*

## ELI SIEGEL
**Author of *Hot Afternoons***
***Have Been in Montana,***

**SECOND EDITION**

New York    DEFINITION PRESS    1965

*The names of the persons in this work are imaginary.
The persons are real.*

Second printing, 1970
Third printing, 1973

# Note to Second Edition

*The Aesthetic Method in Self-Conflict,* originally published in the spring of 1946 and reprinted later the same year, has historical importance as the first publication embodying the philosophy of Aesthetic Realism, founded by Eli Siegel in the early 1940's. It is perhaps the most compact and comprehensive introduction to an understanding of Siegel's central idea: "The world, art, and self explain each other: each is the aesthetic oneness of opposites."

An earlier phrasing of this idea—a phrasing which dates from 1941—was printed on the back cover of the first edition of *The Aesthetic Method:* "The resolution of conflict in self is like the making one of opposites in art."

The present edition is a photographic reproduction of the original, with one editorial change. The term, Aesthetic Analysis, was found to carry too narrow a connotation, and in 1948, Aesthetic Realism was adopted as more exactly descriptive of the philosophy. The author's preface, in which some of the difficulties of nomenclature are discussed, is as it was written in 1946; but in the text itself, Aesthetic Analysis has been changed to Aesthetic Realism.

MARTHA BAIRD, *for*
DEFINITION PRESS

1965

# Preface

This is the first publication of Aesthetic Analysis. Aesthetic Analysis looks on mind as an object like any other object. We believe that what makes for organization of mind is like what makes for organization of a city, a book, a symphony, a store.

The word "self-conflict" is used in the title. It has been found useful to avoid terms of too narrow a medical connotation. Aesthetic Analysis is not medicine or psychiatry in the current sense. Still, it is well to regard self-conflict as meaning "neurosis," when that word is given scope enough and precision enough.

Aesthetic Analysis is practical, for the problem of the integration of self is most unquestionably "practical." It is the "practical problem" beneath all decisions of everyday life. And the first thing necessary in dealing with a practical problem is to see it rightly. There must be seeing before there is remedy.

In our method, the problem of problems, the major, constant, underlying, inevitable thing to organize, deal with sensibly, is: Self and World. However philosophical this phrase may sound, it concerns everyone in the U. S. census or any other census or possible census. Everyone is confronted with, has, the job of: I and All That. Others might call it "one's self and one's environment" or "the individual and society."

Where self-conflict exists or nervousness does, it arises from some inefficient or incomplete or ugly dealing with this problem beneath problems: I and All That; or I and Things; or I and All They. (This is the problem one's talking about when one asks: "How's the world treating you?") To see the question meeting everyone as anything smaller, is unwise.

In Aesthetic Analysis, inward sexual hindrances and "anxiety" and "inferiority" and an untoward "death instinct" are phases or manifestations of the larger problem. If a person's relation with everything which is not himself is sensible, so far will the way he sees sex be sensible. One universe preceded one woman or one man.

In this publication of Aesthetic Analysis, aesthetics itself is the chief matter. In other, coming publications, the general subject will be dealt with otherwise. For example, for a self to separate from the outside world means guilt. The separation can also make for symptoms of a physiological kind: in Aesthetic Analysis the separation is dealt with directly, not the symptoms as such. However, where a self is not at one with the world, is separated from it, the situation is also ugly, against aesthetics in that deep, sober meaning which aesthetics has. And Aesthetic Analysis combats the acquisition in economics which, being a manifestation of self against world or others, makes for disintegration and weakening of personality.

I have elsewhere shown how the unconscious disjunction of a person from the world about him makes for guilt, anger, fear. I have also dealt with how separation from the world has to do with stuttering, insomnia; digestive, menstrual, and other difficulties. Further, the attitude of a person to what is not himself affects what he does in sex; and this matter has also been a subject of Aesthetic Analysis examination. It should be remarked here that Aesthetic Analysis is not merely abstract. Documents exist showing how very precise and earthy it can be. Certain of these documents will be published.

For a fair consideration of this publication, a person

6

must put aside probable previous associations with "aesthetics." Were there a word as exact as aesthetics for the purpose, we would have been glad to use it. The nearest word, other than aesthetics, is dialectics. Dialectics, however, would not express as much as aesthetics does. Terms like Ethical Analysis, Philosophical Analysis, Reality Analysis, we have likewise seen as deficient in one way or another.

It is hoped that Aesthetic Analysis will be seen for what it is: nothing less and nothing more. The method does things to people of a most discernible kind. It has helped to organize lives. It is hoped that before some phrase like "abstract," "impractical," or "I know all that," is used, there will be more seeing—plain seeing. The present pamphlet we hope may serve as a beginning of that seeing.

ELI SIEGEL.


P.S.—We have included "Author of *Hot Afternoons Have Been in Montana*" on the title page. The reason is that this poem, which won the *Nation* Poetry Prize of 1925, is, as we see it, a precursor, in fact, a "first publication" of the Aesthetic Analysis of now. For example:

... There are millions of men in the world, and each
    is one man;
  Each is one man by himself, taking care of himself
    all the time, and changing other men and
    being changed by them;
  The quiet of this afternoon is strange, haunting,
    awful. ...

E. S.

# The Aesthetic Method in Self-Conflict

TOM, Dick, and Harry: Brown, Jones, and Robinson; Hilda, Hulda, and Matilda; little Johnny, tiny Eva and wee Dickie; and the man or girl you know—all have problems by being alive. Aesthetic Realism says that in all of them, and in all persons, tough and genteel, hard-boiled and dreamy, vulgar and elegant, the beginning, large problem is aesthetic: just that.

There is a deep and "dialectic" duality facing every human being, which can be put this way: How is he to be entirely himself, and yet be fair to that world which he does not see as himself? The definition of aesthetics is to be found in a proper appreciation of this duality.

We all of us start with a *here,* ever so snug and ever so immediate. And this *here* is surrounded strangely, endlessly, by a *there.* We are always meeting this *there:* in other words, we are always meeting what is not ourselves, and we have to do something about it. We have to be ourselves, and give to this great and diversified *there,* which is not ourselves, what it deserves. This means we have to be personal and impersonal, snug and exterior. If we do this successfully, whether we know it or not, we have arrived at a beauty which is efficient; at aesthetic good sense. Psychiatrists, should they go about their business completely, boldly, clearly, would be trying to attain this aesthetic propriety and wonder of human behavior.

For psychiatrists do tell persons to be "objective." These psychiatrists certainly would also tell their patients to be "themselves," to have their own opinions, to have lives of their own. What this psychiatric advice really comes to is that people want to be "subjective," too. Therefore, people have to be "objective" and "subjective." Should they be objective one hour and subjective the next hour? Should they be objective about *this* and subjective about *that?* It is not good, it appears, to be shuttling from the factual point of view to the personal point of view. What is left from all this? The following: That a person should, for his mind's health and his deep contentment and his profound efficiency, be objective and subjective at the same time. If he is, he will be aesthetic—for aesthetic means, having an adequate, alive, "personal" perception, while giving oneself truly to the fact outside, the specific reality, the *that.*

There is conflict in most minds as to "personal" and "impersonal," "subjective" and "objective," *here* and *there.*

T HE idea of conflict is essential in any concept of an ailing mind or an ailing self. Were mind or self to be one, it would be sane; where it is not one there is lack of saneness or wholeness; that is, conflict. Conflict as such, in every instance, has two phases to it: there is separateness and there is togetherness. If things in conflict were separate only, they would be too remote to disturb each other; therefore, all would be well. On the other hand, if things in conflict were together only, they would be one; and again all would be well.

To make concrete the rather abstract language of the last paragraph:A girl, Edith, has a sick father whom she does not care for too much but whom, after all, she sees as a father. She thinks of leaving him and she also sees it as her duty to take care of him. These two thoughts are, of course, in conflict; they make up a typical mental field of war. When we look at these thoughts we see that they are together. When Edith thinks of one she may, the next moment, think of the other; she finds reasons for the justice of both. They are like a team of horses which insist on biting and interfering with each other. But a team of unruly horses are definitely together. Yet if they were together in the full sense they would be an orderly team; therefore there is something else than togetherness; there is separateness or opposition.

What emerges, then, is a simultaneity of conspicuous togetherness and conspicuous separateness or opposition. A situation of mind in which there is unavoidable togetherness and unavoidable separateness or opposition, is a conflict.

The basic conflict in the human mind—present, I believe, in all particular conflicts—is that between a person warmly existing to his finger tips, and that person as related to indefinite outsideness: this is the subject and object conflict, the personal and impersonal conflict, the Self and World conflict. In every person there is a drive towards the caring for and pleasing of self; in every person there is a drive towards other things, a desire to meet and know these. Often this drive towards self as an exclusive thing collides painfully with the drive to widen the self. The drives co-exist, that is, they are together; the drives also can be seen as apart, that is, they are separate.

These two drives have their likenesses in art; for at a time of aesthetic activity, a person wants to show his own feelings in a painting, novel, or poem, even if it means lessening objects just as they are; and he also wants to see these objects without imposing narrow desires of self making for its comfort or premature complacency. When an artist is successful, he does not deny either one of these drives, for each is essential; each has its necessity; even its

11

inevitability. But he is not lopsided; he does not accent one, and muffle or curtail the other. The perfect work of art is that where the artist, while entirely himself, while a unique individual, also sees an object in its completeness and precision. If it is possible; if, in fact, it is the great purpose of art to be one's self and yet give everything to the object—can we not find here the just purpose in life itself?

I have observed that in every conflict there is no side which is to be suppressed. The person suffering with a conflict, trying to come to peace, has a tendency to say of a Tuesday: "To hell with *this*"; and on the next day, or for that matter, in the next hour, to say: "To hell with *that*." A neurotic, somewhat jocosely, yet with precision, can be described as a person who makes a loud outcry over losing something which he does not wish to find. He rings door-bells hoping no one is at home.

The neurotic does not wish to destroy either opposing side of his conflict. Still he knows that one side of himself stops him from being at peace with the other; therefore he curses now one, now the other. But even while he outwardly curses something, deeply he hangs on to it. What he needs to do is to see that in having one essential aspect of himself, he need not get rid of the other.


WELL, just that thing: having one attitude and also its opposite, is to be seen in art. If an artist felt that in presenting his feelings intensely, he had to be against seeing an object as it was; if in being excited, he had to neglect calm form—or, put more generally, if he felt that to be his individual self, he had to keep from seeing the outside universe—then the artist would be neurotic, too.

12

Some artists are, but this is not because they're artists, but because they're incomplete artists.

Aesthetics is related to every particular conflict; to everyday conflict. Aesthetics is related to the problems of the ordinary man, the tough guy, the people we meet in our homes, in theatres, in streets, in stores.

For example, there is Harold Jamison of Wilkes-Barre, Pa. Jamison is undergoing a basic, run-of-the-mill conflict. However, what is in his mind, and the possibility of making serene good sense out of it, are of the very heart of psychiatric method. And the only way of making serene good sense out of what's on Jamison's mind, is to make aesthetics out of it. He most likely has had very little to do with the word, maybe he hasn't heard of it; but if Jamison is to walk confidently and sleep well, aesthetics will come to his incompletely articulate mind.

Look at Jamison. He is shy and he is arrogant; in fact, he is like most people. Sometimes, Jamison looks at himself and finds a person who is timid, wants to evade people, thinks people don't like him; is unassertive and inferior. At other times, Jamison is raring to go, feels like an excited regiment, and like a dozen energetic lions up to something. In other words, Jamison of Wilkes-Barre feels both inferior and superior; and when he feels superior, it's hard for him to realize he ever felt inferior. (This also is common.) So the inferiority and superiority feelings of Harold Jamison are in conflict. If he were to visit a mental practitioner in a mood which made him despise wife, children, relatives, and fellow office-workers, of course the practitioner would advise his visitor to get rid of something like narcissism, megalomania, autistic thinking, or the lack of an objective attitude to people.

If, however, Harold Jamison, of a Thursday, feeling

depressed, shy, ashamed, and timorous, were to visit a practitioner, he would be told to get more confidence in himself; to be abased no longer; to walk about proudly and confidently. It might not happen just this way; but I have noticed that mental counselors have told persons to be both less narcissistic and more confident. This may be done subtly, quietly; but it is confusing. How, after all, is one to be full of confidence in himself, and yet not the least bit "narcissistic"? How is one to be deferential, obliging, at times yielding to other people, without being the least bit "dependent" or inferior? This question has to be answered straight; without terminological curlicues or erudite evasiveness. Mr. Jamison, it is clear, has to be both modest and proud—and at the same time, too. He can't be submissive at 4 P.M. and tyrannical at 5 P.M. Well, if the Mr. Jamisons of Wilkes-Barre and the rest of the United States are to be "adjusted" when it comes to their inferiority and superiority ambivalence, it won't be by means of a mental therapy which in itself is contradictory.

AESTHETICS makes the essential superiority and inferiority feelings in man a working team, a team of oneness. We can't kick out either Jamison's arrogance or his shyness. They are both part of him. They are to be made one, and they can be. Right now, they are in conflict; that is, submissiveness and domineeringness are close in Jamison's mind, and yet they are separate. Mr. Jamison wants them to be close; he also wants them to go away from each other. Togetherness is fighting separation in his mind. He is having a bad time.

Aesthetics here should be seen as a possible job of engineering. It is clear that Jamison has to feel yielding and

14

managing at once. Otherwise, he will shuttle unhealthily. The question Jamison and other people face is: Can, in one mind, feelings represented by superiority exist with feelings represented by inferiority? Can we be both humble and bold at 3:30 P.M., Tuesday?—Only art shows that the answer is, Yes. If metaphysics, logic, ethics, psychology, can say yes, too—it's because they are, this while, what art is.

Take Whitman's *Song of Myself.* Whitman yields himself to what he sees; to earth, to people; and he is proud doing so. Art shows we can be proud in seeing clearly, without rigmarole, or pretense, that we are less than we can be. Art makes for pride in the fact, even when that fact is against ego in the narrow sense, or 2-A. (Self having false importance by being opposed to the world is termed by us 2-A.) In Whitman's *Song of Myself*, a man becomes exultant through modesty, modest through exultation. The intense, wide, great fact sweeps Whitman truly; he yields and he has a feeling of deep independence and pride. Where even a Whitman does not feel this, it's because art is not complete. As far as Whitman is an artist—and this is very far; and as far as he gives himself, without interior vanity wriggling, to what is, he feels that *he* is, and he is proud. Jamison should know this.

If a person feels inferior, the first question to ask is, What does he feel inferior about? I don't believe that psychiatrists have asked this question rightly. If a person is unable to do something, or if he doesn't know something, and he knows this neatly, definitely, he will not feel inferior in the morbid sense. He would feel at least he knew himself; and would be proud of that. In other words, in yielding to the facts about himself courageously, truly, there would be a self-approval. Further, if what he desired were good, and he really desired it, he would also approve of himself. Every true desire has action going with it. In following, honestly, steadily, without trickery, a true desire, we feel proud. All this means: yielding to the facts can make us proud.

In aesthetics, there is more true yielding to the facts than elsewhere. Suppose a writer were confessing in his manuscript something which was actually so, and offhand seemed depreciating of him. Having the courage to say what was true of himself, for the purpose of saying it truly and having it known as it was—would he not feel proud? The real critical feeling is always proud: whether of oneself or of others. The real critical feeling, however, seldom occurs.

If knowing oneself were to make inevitably for inferiority, certainly many people should be told not to know themselves. But even the most gentle psychotherapists would hesitate to say people should not know themselves. Behind this hesitation is the feeling that when people know themselves, they truly can approve of themselves because they know what they are. *No self can truly know itself and be ashamed.*

WHEN a self knows what it is, wholly as an object, the thing felt is also the thing feeling. Jamison, deeply, deeply, is after this. If he reaches it, he will be doing the aesthetic thing. For in aesthetics, the self finds its freedom by seeing what it is as an object like other objects; and while there is this seeing, there is the healthy, intense, tremendous feeling of the self as existing, acting, free. The subject has become free by meeting the object wholly. You find this in a baby who knows it's Edgar at fifteen months, because it has met enough objects with not too much of the corruption which later may take place.

Inferiority is really guilt. It doesn't come from your job, as such, or wife, or family, or your acquaintances and friends. Jamison is looking either upon the world as a thing to conquer, handle, exploit, or upon himself as someone to be punished for wanting to be monarchical. This is what goes on deeply. Jamison thinks by respecting something else, *he* is less Jamison. It isn't true; only aesthetics can make it entirely not seem true.

It is difficult really to welcome and use art wholly. A person can't be aesthetic without giving his perceptions entirely to the world. He can't be an arrogant, acquisitive self; and as life now is, it is so easy to want to be. Yet it often happens—and in most lives—that in a person's being really modest, he is proud; that, in a successful not-imposing of himself on objects, he has a sense of well-being.

Suppose we take Rosalind Hines, honestly listening to great music. Rosalind has her interior mishaps, and her inward insufficiencies. Still, something in her wants to listen to Mozart as Mozart, music as music, with the possibly acquisitive Rosalind Hines out of it for a while. An eighteenth century Austrian affects her (the world had affected him). Through Mozart, Rosalind sees the universe for a while come into form in the concert hall. The music has taken her; form and earth have taken her. She yields. She also feels free and proud. In proportion as she is stirred, swept, moved about by sound in great, wonderful order, she is *more* Rosalind Hines, not less.

It is hard, however, while being deeply affected by things to feel we have ourselves intactly. Even Rosalind may have some unconscious qualms after the great Mozartian conquest of her mind. "What happened to me?"

17

she may ask unknowingly to herself. "If this strange external force can do so much to me, where am I, just I?" It is easier, though, to yield to something like music than to something which can more readily and plainly question the complacent and hidden ego. Even so, persons often do not like the fact that music moves them deeply; does something to them unmistakably, thoroughly.

This job of taking care of the warm "oneself" while doing justice to other matters, is truly too philosophic a job for the present day psychiatric equipment. Persons advising other persons will say, in an effort to stabilize selves: "Be yourself"; "Assert yourself." They will also say: "Be interested in other people"; "Think more of other people." When a psychotherapist talks this way, he is affirming conflict; for what a man wants to know is *just how* he can be himself, assert himself, and at the same time be considerate and think more of other people.

L OUIS Robinson, for example, of Syracuse, New York, like all people, talks to, with, and about himself. Sometimes, in these thoroughly intimate conversations, Louis Robinson asserts: "To hell with other people; I'm out for Number One." On other occasions, the somewhat civilized Mr. Robinson says: "This is too bad, thinking of myself all the time; why don't I forget myself and become interested in other things?"

Should a psychiatrist point out "narcissistic trends" in Mr. Robinson's interior cogitations, he's really telling something in technical language which Mr. Robinson has agonizingly known all along. Sometimes, it *has* seemed best to forget other people, and to concentrate energetically on his own well-being, comfort, importance. It seemed to be the one thing to do. What the soul of Louis Robinson is after knowing is, just how he is to be himself and yet give what is coming to all else. A psychiatrist might likewise point out "masochistic" or "inferiority" feelings in Mr. Robinson, for sometimes the Syracuse man feels humble and wants people to help him, and wants to be nice to people, and wants to be punished for not being nice. Therefore, as to Mr. Robinson: advice given to him either that he assert himself or think less of himself, only prolongs the see-sawing existence of the assertive and deferential sufferer. If a way were shown to Louis Robinson—and this would be the one useful kind of advice—by which he could be himself proudly *by* giving everything that was coming to them to other people and things—that way would be aesthetic: nothing less.

Harold Jamison and Louis Robinson are meeting the same troubles. Harold Jamison has what Louis Robinson has; and self-difficulties are present in Wilkes-Barre and in Syracuse. The instance of Jamison shows the dilemma in terms of power and weakness; that of Robinson, in terms of selfishness and unselfishness, injustice and justice. Still, the Jamison situation and the Robinson situation are akin.

Opposites, therefore, are to be put together in lives in Wilkes-Barre and lives in Syracuse; and lives, of course, elsewhere. An artist puts opposites together; a psychiatrist aims, or should aim, to put personality opposites together. If a psychiatrist succeeds in putting elements in basic opposition together, he would be doing as an artist does.

Where opposites exist, and are not one, there is conflict. Every kind of conflict is, in principle, alike. Opposites in the self are not made by us; we have them by being alive. How our opposites are in relation shows itself in what we do; in the manifestations of daily life. We all of us begin with our selves, and our selves have opposites. It is possible they will work against each other—this is what most largely happens; it is also possible they will be integrated, together, a one.

A PERSON is separate from all other things and together with all other things. To understand opposites in a self, the meaning of *together* and *separate* must be seen. (This meaning is like that of *same* and *different*.) The meaning may seem abstract, and may seem hardly worth going after by a psychiatrist; yet if he fails to go after it, he is evading the entirety of his function. All art puts *separateness* and *togetherness* together. All selves want to do this.

Take a common instance showing the *separate* and *together* problem. Five household objects are in a corner of a moving van. They are seen by a boy, Albert. They are a clock, a table, a chair, a bed, and a lamp. These objects are huddled together in a corner. Albert doesn't think they look proper or good, and hardly anyone would think so. They are close together, all right. But their closeness makes for clashing. The lamp seems to interfere with the bed by hanging right over it; the clock is on the chair, and doesn't belong there; and the table has the bed right up against it. Yes, the things are near to each other; you could almost say they hug each other; but it's their nearness that seems to make them fight. Albert doesn't like the looks of the five objects; even though he wouldn't say it was a bad arrangement of separateness and togetherness.

And then the things in the moving van reach Albert's home. They are put carefully in a room. The bed is farther away from the table; and the lamp is not so near the bed; and the clock is far from the chair. But Albert likes the way they look, better. What has happened is, that because the objects are more separate in a certain way, they are more together. They are close because they're apart. In other words, separateness is not fighting togetherness.

All of us, in a way, are separate from the world. We seem to end with our bodies. If our neighbor, only half a foot away, has a nail in his shoe, we might know about it; but we don't feel it the way he does. If a bed companion blows his nose, our nose is unblown. A blister on a finger touching ours is not our blister. And we seem to have a whole secret manufactory of all kinds of views, impressions, perceptions, outlooks, considerations, desires —all for ourselves, alone. So we are alone in our blood and our bones and our thoughts. It seems we are separate, if we want to feel that way.

And yet we can look out. Not a thing fails to act on us, once we think about it. To think about something means that it acts on us; for when our thoughts are about anything, this thing has changed our minds. We cannot live without ever so many objects, from everywhere. The ground we walk on is unthinkable as not being. Our food is a neighbor which becomes ourselves. The air is a universal indispensable. And we need people. We may even need them to despise them. Everything is around us, indefinitely close, indefinitely inescapable, indefinitely changing ourselves, becoming ourselves. This means we are not only *separate*, we are *together*.

When things are well or beautifully arranged, in every instance, the side of them which can be seen as separate goes

21

along rightly with the side of them which can be seen as together. We saw this with the five objects first in the moving van and then in the room. No matter how many objects are concerned, two, and only two, opposite things are involved. When we talk of the composition of materials, say, the problem is how to place these materials so that their separateness does not conflict with their togetherness. For *all* objects can be seen as being away from other objects, discordant with them; or as close to them, mingling with them serenely.

SO the problem that faces a self is how to make its separateness at one with its togetherness. This is the problem which is underneath all others. It can make for agony and it can make for triumph; it can make for painful jumpiness or mobile composure.

There were five objects involved in the first instance I gave of everyday composition. The following is an instance of two objects: A drum and a clarinet are playing at once. The way they play is plainly different. If the drum tries to play exactly what the clarinet is playing, the result is not good. If the drum plays something too different, wrongly opposed to what the clarinet is playing, the result isn't good, either. It would be disastrous if the clarinet were playing *Tales of the Vienna Woods* and the drum were doing something with *Turkey in the Straw*. It would be disastrous also if the clarinet were playing *Turkey in the Straw* and the drum playing, as much as possible, *Turkey in the Straw* the same way. In the first instance of disaster, separateness would be working against togetherness; in the second instance, infelicity would come from togetherness as against separateness. Still, it is possible that, as can be seen very often in halls where music is played, the clarinet and drum can play different things at the same time (or, if one prefers, play different ways); and it is possible that the difference *make* for togetherness or harmony. In all beautiful arrangements, difference works with sameness, separateness with togetherness.

According to Aesthetic Realism, the self is trying to come into composition with the world, and at the same time be different, individual, separate, free. In the instance of drum and clarinet playing well, the clarinet could be seen as helping the drum and the drum as helping the clarinet; that is, the drum could be seen as independent while having the clarinet help it, and the clarinet independent while having the drum help it.

The world *is* helped by our being in it, for without our personalities, the world would not have used every possibility it has; and the world can be seen as helping us. The fact that we need the world does not mean that we are not free; for when we need something to be free, the need is not disabling.

We can see ourselves as separate from, and as together with, the world. When we see our separateness simultaneously with our togetherness, and working as a neat team, or as one, we are adjusted aesthetically, that is, really. For every self can see what it is, at once as separate, together, and both.

There is aesthetics in numbers. The self can be likened to an addition or a subtraction. In us, always, things are added, subtracted; included, put aside. The two sides of us can be seen as two numbers present in us. We can call these numbers 5 and 7. In the neurotic mind, the presence of 5 is in tormenting conflict with the presence of 7. The unstable person thinks that in accepting 5, he must do away with 7; and in welcoming 7, he must banish 5. So, at times, he welcomes 5 and shows 7 the door. But 7 still persists in being around. So he greets 7 warmly and acts coldly to 5. But 5 won't stay away either, for long. Under many disguises, with many transformations, with many embodiments in ordinary life, this shuttling, fickleness, indecision, is what goes on in the nervous person.

Now 5 and 7 must both exist. They are both indispensable. Neither can be seen as not present; neither can be shown the door. The question is, how can both be welcomed? How can the separateness and the togetherness be, at once, neatly maintained?

Simply by seeing them together as 12. Suppose 5 and 7 are seen as 12. You can see 5 separately in 12. You can see the disturbing elements of 5 destroyed, because when 5 has added 7 to it, 5 is destroyed by becoming 12. You also can see 5 as completed by becoming 12. Furthermore, you can see 7 separately in 12. You can see 7 as destroyed by having 5 added to it, and changed into 12. You can also see 7 as completed by having 5 added to it. And, as I said, you can see 7 and 5 quietly, harmoniously, serenely, as one, in 12.

The destruction of 5 by 7 in 12 is an aspect of the separateness of 7. The destruction of 7 by 5 in 12 is an aspect of the separateness of 5. When these numbers become 12, they can be seen also as together. And when a number is seen as completed by the other, there is also separateness with completeness. Anyway, the making of two warring numbers, 7 and 5, into 12, implies separateness and togetherness working together. Here mathematics can be seen as art.

If, instead of the numbers 5 and 7, deep notions of freedom and security are troubling a person, the solution is the

24

same. A neurotic cannot feel he can be free and secure at once; he does not feel he can be free while accepting "discipline" or security.

Timothy Watkins wants to feel he can do as he pleases; that he can relax just like that; that he does not have to put his nose to the grindstone constantly. Yes, Timothy Watkins is against what he sees as restrictions. But, troublesomely, Mr. Watkins finds also that he wants order and routine; that if he does not do something at a specific time, he doesn't feel so good; and that the notion of insecurity frightens him; and the lack of a "system" irks him. And he feels that if he "plugs" for freedom, routine will go to the dogs, or worse; and he will be a disorganized person. Yet he feels, too, that if he chooses routine unquestionably, he will lose his personality; will be smothered by a pattern; crushed by a grind; become a dull human mechanism.

The question confronting everyone is: Is it possible for a human being to do truly as he pleases, to give adequate regard to the intense uniqueness of the moment, to show his instincts (including the primeval), his impulses, his drives, his untrammeled personality—and at the same time satisfy his sense of order, of precision, of stability, of responsibility, of justice? Aesthetic Realism says, Yes; and wants the yes implemented.

For, if the world does not permit freedom and routine to function simultaneously, while making a person want both, it is profoundly inviting ethical chaos, psychic disturbance, universal neurosis. An agonizing see-saw would follow; the world would be unjust. The drive towards freedom and the drive towards precision exist deeply and permanently in the human being: neither can be eradicated; neither can be played off against the other; neither should be nor has to be.

25

Lacking the aesthetic attitude, persons sometimes lop off some of the drive towards freedom, sometimes lop off some of the drive towards order. Persons vary from the rippling, blown wave to the fixed rock. There is a sad shuttling through life. It should be seen that none of the basic impulses is bad. The discomfort does not come from the impulse itself, but from its disproportionate setting off against another impulse. Who would say that freedom is a bad thing? Who would say that order is a bad thing? Who would say that these weren't basic states of the human mind? If eye and toe can go together in a human body, why can't abandon and restraint?

The only reason why people think that freedom and order can't go together is because they look on opposites necessarily as antagonistic, not as useful to each other, or kind to each other. Negative and positive in the electron are opposed to each other, but they certainly couldn't get along without each other; they certainly are inter-helpful. Woman and man are in a sense opposed to each other, but they certainly can be useful to each other. Sky and ocean are quite different, but there is a kind of general assistance given by one to the other.

One of the most necessary alterations of the present day human mind, is the changing of the feeling that opposites have to fight, that they can't exist as one. Many, many people seeing opposing drives in their minds, feel they have to choose one or the other; and curse the one they don't choose. This is deeply foolish, but it goes on in every State of the Union, and elsewhere.

Aesthetics is not foolish in this way. It points to glorious good sense. It points to an exciting friendship of different ways of mind. Every aesthetic thing, or beautiful thing, or artistic thing, has freedom and order; has to have it, or

26

it wouldn't be aesthetic. A beautiful thing made by man shows that the world gives persons an unlimited chance for tingling good sense. Does a great painting have freedom and order? If a painting didn't have freedom in it, could we call it great? If it didn't have order in it, could we call it great? Does it have freedom at 4:10 P.M. and order at 4:20? Hardly. It has freedom and order at once. And one feels like asking, What is it that painting—coming from the human mind—can do which the human mind itself can't do? A person can ask about a picture, What has it got I can't have—or shouldn't have?

A novel, in essence, has the same thing as a painting. A novel is one thing and many things, that is, it is a whole and parts. And whole and parts are working together. In a good novel you see a certain precision, "has-to-be-ness," or inevitability—that is, there is order in a good novel. And in a novel, too, you feel the characters act freely, the writer is not constrained; there is growth and there is strangeness in the novel: what this means is, the novel has freedom. The freedom and order are to be seen in every chapter; indeed, they can be seen in every sentence. Freedom and order, in a good novel, have their hands, in friendly fashion, on each other's shoulders.

IT can be said definitely that wherever there is composition making for beauty, the problem of the neurotic mind is solved in outline. Even if the composition is in a very small field, that presence of freedom and order at once can be seen. Perhaps this can best be exemplified in a single line of poetry. I choose a line from Shelley's *Ode to the West Wind*:

Oh lift me as a wave, a leaf, a cloud!

27

This line has a definite order: in a certain sense it is as definite as bookkeeping. It has ten syllables. These syllables can be divided into five pairs of two each. The first syllable of each pair is unaccented. The second is accented. (So the line can be read, though some might demur at accenting the word *as*. The demur here I think is incorrect.) The line is what is technically called an iambic pentameter; that is, a line of ten syllables, five feet, with the accent falling on each second syllable.

With metrical scansion, the line appears as:

Oh *lift* | me *as* | a *wave,* | a *leaf,* | a *cloud!*

The line arranged this way still has all its freedom. There is a metrical beat, a pause, on the word *lift;* on the word *as;* on the word *wave;* on the word *leaf;* on the word *cloud.* Yet there is motion in the word *lift;* there is uncertainty in the word *as;* there are ripplingness and speedy curve in the word *wave;* there are height and lightness in the word *leaf;* and there are greater height and airiness in the word *cloud.* The line rises from the word *lift.* There is a going towards the sky from the word *wave.* All this happens *while* the words themselves, like grenadiers, or bricks, or pillars, are precise, fixed, methodical, even statistical. All this comes to the fact that in the line of Shelley I have quoted, the mind of man can find security and adventure, exactness and unrestraint. The line is, in the best sense, mightily adjusted; all the psychiatrists in America can learn from it.

A great deal has been said of the closeness of life to art. The question is, whether art gives order, intensifies life, makes it greater. If art makes life greater, cannot what is in art be used as a means of making life more sensible? Life in other words, makes art; cannot art be used in turn on life; and how?

There is no limit to how art can be used to make life more sensible.  To see art as making life more sensible it is first required of one that he respect art, know what it is, not make it less than it is.

Art, Aesthetic Realism believes, shows reality as it is, deeply: straight.  All art does that.  The possibilities of reality *are* reality.  The more we see reality as having order and strangeness, form and wonder, the more reality we are seeing.  Art is a way of seeing reality more by seeing it more as it is.

It is well at this point to take another line of verse, another iambic pentameter.  The line is:


The twisted branches of the knotted oak.


This line has the same meter as the line of Shelley.  The feeling or substance of it is different.  It doesn't go swiftly to the skies.  Its motion is different.  Presented metrically, the line is:


The *twist* | ed *bran* | ches *of* | the *knot* | ted *oak.*


Again, there is order.  The accented syllables fall regularly.  There is a statistical division in the line.  Still, the line goes all over the place.  It seems confused.  It is twisting.  It curves.  It has knots.  It seems to be against symmetry.  But symmetry is there.  The words like *twisted, knotted, branches,* even, are placed in terms of sound with precision.  In listening to the line we hear precision and

29

helter-skelterness at once, confusion and correct number-ing. The question is, whether the line's being both con-fused and precise is of reality.

It is. Is not reality confused and orderly at once? Does it not have storms and crystals? Are there not jungles and ordered grass? Isn't the body of an animal organized and changeable? Isn't the sky fixed and moody? Don't events occur both by law and with unpredictability? Isn't the world limited and unlimited? Doesn't mind go by cause and effect, and yet strangely? Isn't everything in reality both strange and definite, existent yet endless?—Well, if reality is two things at once, if a poetic line is two things at once, can't we say that the "dilemma" quality in reality is captured, dealt with wisely, in a line of good verse?

Aesthetic Realism believes that reality as such is aes-thetic: that is, it is both free and definite. If we don't see it that way, we are not seeing reality as it is. And since the purpose of psychiatry is to see reality as it is, it should be the purpose of psychiatry to have people (including psychiatrists) see reality as being logical beauty.

All the problems in aesthetics are of immediate, lasting importance for mind. Every aesthetic question is a "must" for human happiness. Let us consider the Shelley line again:

Oh lift me as a wave, a leaf, a cloud!

Suppose I change the line to:

Pray elevate me as if I were a wave, or a leaf, or a cloud.

It will be seen that by making the line more relaxed, more diffused—less definite—I have also taken away the "lift" or freedom in it. The freedom in the Shelley line depends on its precision, its economy. By altering the precision, adding superfluity, I have taken away the speed, the ardor, the might in motion of the line. Too much in the way of words here makes for too little. The music is gone. Style has left; and with it, the great good sense the line had.—And aesthetic mistakes or deficiencies are like life mistakes or deficiencies. All "adjustment" is a rhythm of definiteness or neatness of self with suggestion or freedom, just as a good line of poetry is.


THE psychiatry of the future will look at art zealously, constantly, with the utmost respect and cognitive love. It will find, for instance, in that separation and togetherness in the tango, a guide to the problem of leaving and remaining, far and near, aloofness and huggingness, there is in the self. Every good dance, every good symphony, every good picture, every good short story, every good ballad, will serve as a guide to what humans want, how they can be richly sane, how they can live truly and with meaning.

Every work of art is a problem in being oneself and being other, being *here* and being *there*. As I have mentioned, the solution of this problem is to be found in the procedure of the tango. When the partners are close to each other, they have in mind the long steps away; there are a constant procession and interaction of intimacy, steppings aside, definite departures. However, the intimacy, the steppings aside, the departures, all have one purpose. They all help each other. There is not a rift among them. Their being different makes them the same in so

31

far as their being different has one end—the order and excitement of the dance.

Beauty has not been respected sufficiently. The word *beauty*, even today, has a delicate, frail ring to it. If you talk about beauty, you are regarded by many as not being tough-minded. This should stop. Beauty has to be seen as complete logic, good sense carried further than usual: resplendent sanity.

The moment when beauty comes to be in a mind, is a moment where unconscious and conscious have met well. Beauty shows what we want; and the unconscious is, most deeply, what we want which we don't know we want. The unconscious is also what we don't want which we don't know we don't want. The unconscious is always looking for an expression or embodiment, which we can *see*. What we haven't been aware of, or what we are not aware of, we become aware of as we give aesthetic form to things. It is important to see that every grammatical sentence has a kind of beauty to it; and that when we freely use a good sentence, or talk with form, the unconscious desire for order in change we have, has been embodied in such a way we can consciously be aware of it.

It is a belief of Aesthetic Realism that the unconscious and conscious are acting together in mid-afternoon when we rather calmly talk of ordinary things to acquaintances; and that the unconscious is every moment of our lives functioning, and possibly functioning with order.

Psychoanalysis has helped to make a disjunction between flesh and form. The sensual has been opposed to the logical. The fact that in a painting of Rubens, say, a fleshly, naked woman can be given form, points to the possibility of seeing the voluptuous as intellectual. The reality that made an attractive body also made possible the logic that may be in a mind looking at that attractive body. One of the purposes of art is to have the intellectual felt concretely, even sensually; and to see the sensual as having possible form. Aesthetic Realism says it is one person who can desire a woman and theorize about cube roots. Aesthetic Realism says that the body of a person functions in both desiring a woman and theorizing about cube roots; and that since the body does, the self does.

No person will be at ease, deeply, or fully happy about sex, unless what his body does is at one with form. Wherever sex makes for division—no matter how much a person may know physiologically about it—it hasn't been seen wholly as it is. Sex in man goes towards aesthetics, and has to go towards it.


I HAVE dealt earlier, with two fairly ordinary human beings. These persons, Harold Jamison and Louis Robinson, had problems which in their largest meaning were the problems all art faces. The same kind of problems is had by Hilda Rawlins, distressed young lady living on Central Park West, Manhattan. Miss Rawlins' distress arises from her not being able to manage the problem of unity and diversity in her. Sometimes, Hilda has a corrupt and intense drive towards the unity, the purity of herself. It is then she doesn't want to see anybody. She wishes to stay in bed. She is not interested in the events of the world, or in the events of her friends' lives. Newspapers, to her, are abhorrent. The idea of seeing a show is repellently remote, hardly to be thought of. The notion of going to a party is painfully impossible. The reason for all this is, that Hilda Rawlins wants to have herself "definitely," unstainedly, unalloyedly. Her unconscious feels that the only way to have herself unpolluted by externalities is to deny externality; spurn it, put it out of her life, even annihilate it.

Still, her larger unconscious self knows that this is no way to attain the unity of personality, no way to integrate, sustain selfhood. For in Miss Rawlins' mind, as in other minds, there is a co-existent tendency towards manyness, the heterogeneous earthiness of things. Hilda isn't calm about this tendency, either; for she sees it as the enemy of the tendency towards unity, and doesn't want to see the two tendencies together.

On June 4th, Hilda went to bed feeling—quite sincerely —ill, and told her mother she did not wish to answer telephone calls, receive visitors, or read letters. Even books were looked on with disfavor by the profoundly recoiling Hilda. She remained in bed until June 9th, talking to no one except her mother, and with her curtly. Glumly, she received medicines given to her by a young lady hired for the occasion. Hilda's bed was her universe, with the addition of a stretch of floor and the bathroom. Outwardly, she wasn't happy; but the narrow unconscious, or 2-A, had taken her over, and that, in its subterranean fashion, was triumphant.

Nevertheless, Hilda, being human, had that in her which needed more than herself. The fight between the two aspects of herself was always going on, and had been going on. On June 9th, the strength of the unconscious forces altered. The fight had been going on, unknown to Hilda. The outcome of the fight, however, seized upon her. On June 9th, Hilda had a sudden desire to see people, to talk to them, to have them near, near to her. She flung the bed clothes off her. She called up friends. She talked

34

buoyantly, raptly. She went out. On the subway, she was interested in everybody. She wanted to grab everybody to herself. If she didn't know *everything* about a person, she felt bad. She was tremendously agog and curious.

At a party, Hilda had a smile for everyone. She asked questions eagerly. She showed untiring interest in everyone to whom she was talking, and she talked to many. She wanted to put her arms around the whole, encyclopedic universe. This breathless participation of Hilda in everything she met went on for four and a half days. Late on June 13th, Hilda felt strangely tired. She went to bed feeling sad. A vague fear was in her mind. She had faintly, but pervasively, a headache.

The next morning, Hilda declined an invitation. She talked somberly to her mother. She was interested in death, and talked about it with Mrs. Rawlins. The next days, Hilda was mournful. She wasn't impolite, as she had been before; but she was confused, waveringly aloof. Once, with her aunt who came to see her, Hilda was abrupt and rude. Ten minutes later, she meekly apologized. Life at this time for Hilda was criss-cross, winding up and down, unformed. She began to think of God, religion, and even thought of going away somewhere to lead a selfless, religious life, doing nothing but helping other people.

Three moods were present in Hilda Rawlins' self. One of these moods was fiercely exclusive; it wanted to achieve ego contentment by keeping out, forgetting, negating. The other was excessively acquisitive, grabbing disproportionately, possessively aware of all things unknown, all things not Hilda. The third was a bad mingling of the first two, making Hilda tired and mournful. In this mood she wanted to present herself "selflessly" to "God"; she could lose her apparent outward self, but have her unconscious

35

ego; the fact that this was not acceptable to her whole personality "slowed" her up.

Had Hilda been aware that she could have herself as one thing, while it was meeting all kinds of situations and persons and objects, Hilda would not have had to stay in bed, would not have had to be rapturously grabbing, and she would not have had to be confusedly, incompletely religious. Hilda's self, like all selves, is an aesthetic proposition. By this I mean the questions she had to answer about what she was, are the questions a working artist has deeply to answer. Hilda asked herself without knowing it—and therefore did not completely ask it— How can I be a unity with detail? How can I be in motion, yet stable? How can I be perfect and imperfect? How can I be known and unknown to myself? How can I be I and other than I? How can I be a changing composition and a fixed singleness?

At every moment in her life, the whole self of Hilda was a definition and a mobility, an intimacy and a remoteness. Hilda's life, however, had made it so that these two aspects of herself were seen as separate selves. Hilda was never able to see, just so, that her meeting of people, her listening to them, her reading of books, was the *means* of having herself as such. Hilda wanted to be Hilda and nothing less, or more; she also wanted to be popular, go out, experience things. She had never asked clearly: Is the Hilda that acts with people *just* the same Hilda that thinks to herself? Is the Hilda under her skin, so warm, so taking-care-of-herself, the same Hilda that laughs at another's joke, pours tea for a strange young man, calls up a publisher on behalf of a good cause? She hadn't asked, was it the same Hilda who allowed her hand to be held by Stan Hayes for fifteen minutes, as the Hilda who thought about Stan Hayes while she was lying in bed? She had never asked was Hilda's Hilda the same as other people's Hilda?

THE self is indefinitely deep and indefinitely extensive. It is vertical and horizontal. It is an ineluctable unity while it is constantly mobile. Hilda had not seen that the deep Hilda was also the extensive Hilda; that her vertical self was also her horizontal self; that the unity of Hilda was also her mobility. She had placed the static aspect of her personality against the dynamic.

There is not a pair of opposites I have used which is not relevant to Hilda's pain and pleasure, depression and exaltation; and also to the procedures and aims of art.

Art is internal and external. The repose a person feels in aesthetic creation comes from his, for the time, feeling he is what he is and also what he is not. Ego and otherness don't fight for the while. The artist feels he has reached form in the deepest places of his personality, because things outside himself have been seen courageously, truly, respectfully by him.

Neuroticism is corrupted knowledge. Art is complete knowledge. There is a tremendous correspondence between the very unlimited depths of personality and the astonishing universe in its suddenness, its ordinariness, its surprisingness, its concreteness, its boundlessness. The depths, the real depths, of self, are the world. The further we know what these depths are, the further we know what reality is. The last point in the unconscious of the human being meets the meaning of an everyday object in its completeness.

37

Could, therefore, Hilda see an inkstand or a friend or the sky utterly, she would be having herself. If she is afraid to meet an object utterly, it is because she is afraid that in doing so, instead of having herself more, she would lose her precise and warm Hilda-ness.

If one meets an object utterly, he sees it with unrestrained verticality and horizontality, definition and comprehensiveness. As our mind goes towards an object, works on it, so our mind is. We are the way we know.

Now Hilda had the vertical aspect of herself and the horizontal. Everyone has. The vertical line is a symbol to the unconscious of the self alone; the horizontal, of the self going out. Our selves go towards the precision of a line seen as nothing—for a line can be thought of as not being at all—that is, simply as a line. The down and up motion of a line is like the ego given to nothing but itself. The horizontal line also is like nothing, but represents the ego going out, as an *off-set* to verticality. Were the vertical line to become one with the horizontal line, narrowness, width, and height would exist at once; and further, were width and height to become one, the motion continued would make for a square, then a cube; and if a point in a line were completed, with both dark and light, it would make a circle.

What I have just written is, of course, abstract. Still, it can be said that the self is a point; a line, both vertical and horizontal; a square; a cube, a triangle; a circle. Somewhere, this is practical.

The personality of everyone is both solidity and space. One way of saying space and solidity is mind and body. At any moment, if we try, we can see our feelings, which are in a sense all we know, like space; they are not solid, as feelings; they can't be touched, as feelings. And we have a body. The feelings of our body, which is ourselves, are form; the body can be seen as weight.

In aesthetics, various geometric forms meet. Solidity and space also become one. In that aspect of ourselves which is our body, it is clear we can find all the forms I have mentioned: a sphere, a cube, a cone. In the space quality of our feelings, we can find all the other forms: the point, the line, the square, the triangle, the circle.

The aesthetic problem I have accented with Hilda Rawlins is that of singleness and manyness, or oneness and diversity. In her, or concerning her, are all other aesthetic problems. The things that make art, go together. If they are present in a person, they are present in their multiplicity and completeness.

I F A person, for example, were to be completely happy, body and form would be entirely at one. The most graceful body acts *as if it were not a body*. When a person is happy, he is likely to say: "I feel light as a feather." However, he knows that he's present to himself and all others in his, perhaps, 160 pounds. In all bodies, there is a tendency to absence of body: that is, form.

Further, it has been said that a completely good digestion would mean one we did not have to be aware of; one we did not have to think about at all. Yet, it is apparent, it would be well for a person having a good digestion to know that he had it. In this situation of being able to be unaware of a bodily state and yet to know that it exists, there is that beautiful combination of naiveté and subtlety, spontaneity and awareness, unconscious and conscious, that makes art.

And then there is the problem of slowness and speed —in everything and everyone. Sometimes, Hilda talks too fast. At other times, words come painfully, draggingly. What this means is that in her there is a warring of basic speed against basic slowness. An aspect of rhythm, or of form in time, is the feeling of speed in slowness, slowness in speed. When music is good, there is a sense of motion and of pause. A play is good when we think things are happening, and yet there is something meditative, large, easy, spatially quiet. When we feel that something is speedy and quiet at once, we feel something beautiful. That is why, if Hilda comes to be entirely "well," she will have put in her personality a presence at once of slowness and speed, meditativeness and agogness, akin to that which we can find in a good concerto, in a good one-act play, in a good bit of choreography, in a good moving picture.

Sometimes, Hilda has yearned for what has been called the "simple life." She also has wanted to be in a constant round of New York social complexities; wanted things to happen; wanted to see new things constantly; wanted to be in a whirl of excitement, going places, even intrigue. Well, this desire for both simplicity and complication is also seen in what art goes after, what it has to meet if it reaches what it goes after. Every work of art has largely succeeded with the problem of simplicity and complexity. Some works accent one, or seem to be one, offhand; but they all have both.

For how can a thing really be simple unless there is a chance, felt somewhere, it could have been, or is, complex, too? Simplicity, without the likelihood of intricacy, would hardly be satisfying. If, for example, a symphony seems complex, it is simple also as much as its complexities have been arranged rightly. And if a song seems simple and is a good or great song, its simplicity must have suggestion, many sides, richness to it, if its simplicity is to be other than thin, pretty-pretty, false.

The self has in it the drive towards simplicity, for it must be one. It has in it the drive towards multiplicity, for the world is various, and the self grows by meeting more and more and arranging this more and more.

It is incumbent, therefore, on Hilda Rawlins, that she feel herself to be as simple as a pebble and as complicated as a Demerara jungle, at once. The self is that way: wants to be that way; has to be that way. The problem of simplicity in the self won't be dealt with sufficiently if Hilda decides to go to some farmhouse, eat cream, avoid complicated books, eschew the telephone, go about in dungarees, and lie on the grass looking at nothing but the blue sky. She won't become really simple by making much of nakedness, "nature," and undisturbed devotion to the soil. That is not the simplicity the human personality is truly satisfied with.

IT SHOULD be asked: Does the self want much diverse experience? Ah yes, in all of us can be discerned, affirmed, a desire to avoid intricacy, to make life as neat, as simple as possible. But if we don't stop looking at ourselves, we can also find a desire for unlimited experience: "for life and more life and yet more life"; for subtle and delicate adventure. These possibilities of the self are both to be met. So what are we going to do? Be simple in the summer and complicated in the fall; avoid intricacy in the morning and welcome spiritual adventure in the afternoon? This won't work. People have tried it and

41

come to dislike themselves for their pains. The metaphysical, or aesthetic obligation faces us of being simple and intricate at the same moment, in the same hour, in the same day, in the same life.

The history of art shows that there is a true beauty in simplicity and a true beauty in complexity. A novel like *Robinson Crusoe* is beautiful. Tolstoi's *War and Peace* is beautiful. The simplicity of the Twenty-third Psalm is good; the ornateness of Swinburne's chorus from *Atalanta,* "When the Hounds of Spring," is good. Complexity, however, is also in Defoe's novel; and simplicity in Tolstoi's multitudinous work. The Twenty-third Psalm has in its plainness a richness, diversity, unexpectedness of rhythm. Swinburne's "When the Hounds of Spring" has, along with its swift ornateness, its flashing changes of rhythm and word, a driving simplicity of structure.

In mind, wherever simplicity does not have richness to it, the simplicity is thin, not real. Our unity must come from a multitudinous welcoming; otherwise it is too easy, exclusive, timid, artificial, unhealthy.

And Hilda has wanted the strange; and she has wanted the homely, the "comfy," the close. She has had thoughts of spending the rest of her life with her mother and a cousin in some neat, unpretentious place. She has also wanted to go to Africa, to Fontainebleau, to Rome, and see the sights and objects there and in other places. She enjoyed having tea and cake with her mother one day, and had a decided yearning to visit the interior of Australia the next.

These things happen: they are a phase of the "realism-romance" problem as it is in the human mind; it is also the problem of ordinariness and strangeness as we find it in the history of art. And all great art or true art is strange and ordinary, wonderful and matter-of-fact; strange, perhaps, because of the *way* it is ordinary; matter-of-fact because of the *way* it is wonderful.

There is not a basic problem that the minds of Harold Jamison, Louis Robinson, and Hilda Rawlins face, which is not deeply, most clearly, a problem of art. When willed beauty—which is art—is understood, it will be seen as always with us, never rightly to be put aside: inevitable. Beauty is good sense. It is hard good sense. It takes all of us in. If we wish to be really well, let us understand it.